Do NOT Stop For Hitchhikers

poems by

Marianne Gambaro

Finishing Line Press
Georgetown, Kentucky

Do NOT Stop For Hitchhikers

Copyright © 2018 by Marianne Gambaro
ISBN 978-1-63534-426-4 First Edition
All rights reserved under International and Pan-American Copyright Conventions. No part of this book may be reproduced in any manner whatsoever without written permission from the publisher, except in the case of brief quotations embodied in critical articles and reviews.

ACKNOWLEDGMENTS

The author wishes to thank the editors of the following journals in which these poems first appeared:

The 5th Annual Writer's Digest Poetry Awards, "Yellowstone in Winter"
Avocet, "The Lupines of Ushuaia"
The Aurorean, "From Robert Frost's Porch"
Blood and Thunder, "Crossing the Lethe" and "The Weathervane"
Oberon, "TripAdvisor"

Publisher: Leah Maines
Editor: Christen Kincaid
Cover Art: Jim Gambaro, jimgambarophotography.zenfolio.com
Author Photo: Jim Gambaro, jimgambarophotography.zenfolio.com
Cover Design: Elizabeth Maines McCleavy

Printed in the USA on acid-free paper.
Order online: www.finishinglinepress.com
         also available on amazon.com

Author inquiries and mail orders:
Finishing Line Press
P. O. Box 1626
Georgetown, Kentucky 40324
U. S. A.

Table of Contents

TripAdvisor 1

The Sisters Visit 2

Yellowstone in Winter 4

Good Dog 5

(Boomers Driving) On the Taos Plateau 7

In the Shadow of the Space Station 8

From Robert Frost's Porch 9

Open Mic at Luthier's 10

How Maria Came to America 11

According to Aunt Rose 12

Euro Mutts 13

First Trip to New York 14

Do NOT Stop for Hitchhikers 15

Elegy for Palisades Amusement Park 17

The End of the Road 19

Bandelier 20

Meteor Crater, Arizona 21

The Weathervane 22

Crossing the Lethe 23

The Hallway that Leads to the Morgue 24

The Boy Up the Street 25

The Lupines of Ushuaia 27

Overheard in the Quiet Car 28

For Jim, my best friend and rudder. In memory of Carl Russo, co-founder of the Florence Poets Society, who kept me writing, even when my muse took time off.

TripAdvisor

There is no category in Expedia
for the journey of the heart.
Not under "hotel," "flight," "restaurant"
or any combination thereof.
It is the longest and the loneliest trip,
but rich with promise and possibilities.
It is aided by neither map nor GPS,
advice and counsel of previous travelers ignored.
No discounted fares are available,
even if your dates are flexible.
No stars or recommendations can guide you.
Some never reach their destination.
Others don't recognize it when they get there.
Was this review helpful?

The Sisters Visit

No sign marks the driveway.
We'd passed it twice.
Not a driveway at all but a hardened dirt trail
through second-growth forest,
punctuated by rocks and ruts and Father's expletives.
Late model two-tone coupe
challenging a frail wooden bridge,
then yet another curve.

Dogs bark in greeting
as we round the final bend.
Close cropped hair,
man's worn red plaid shirt and dungarees,
my aunt pauses her rake
from smoothing the gravel as if laying
a red carpet for royal guests.
Father parks our gleaming Oldsmobile
next to their rusting station wagon.
Black-eyed Susans and Queen Anne's lace
decorate weathered clapboard.

Canning jars line the kitchen counter
with Technicolor reds and greens and saffrons.
Mother silently bunny lips her unease
as she gingerly sits on the edge of the worn sofa
unconsciously smoothing her skirt
which will go to the drycleaner's first thing Monday morning.
Her back to the snake in the terrarium,
she watches with barely concealed horror
as a turtle moseys across the floor
toward the cast iron skillet of ground beef
he shares with the dogs.

Sun brewed ice tea with still-warm mint.
Oatmeal cookies freshly baked for guests.
We stay the minimum
departing with perfunctory kisses, awkward hugs
and promises to call.

Safely out of earshot Mother asks
> *How can my sister live like that?*

I think
> *How could she not?*

Yellowstone in Winter

As geysers blow and sputter in the snow
the bison graze within a field of steam.
The scene remains unchanged from long ago.
It's all a part of nature's greater scheme.

The summer tourists flee this vast extreme
where trees stand black against the white tableau.
The silence shatters to an eagle's scream
as geysers blow and sputter in the snow.

The icy vises break where thermals flow,
and cygnets glide the river's course downstream.
Near geysers where the fragile grasses grow
the bison graze within a field of steam.

No heat is transferred from the sun's bright beam.
At dusk the moon recasts its icy glow
on shadows even denser than they seem.
The scene remains unchanged from long ago.

An elk upon a windswept high plateau
with nerves on edge surveys the winter scene.
Her calf's remains yield fodder for the crow.
It's all a part of nature's greater scheme.

The grizzly sows bear even as they dream,
their sleep unbroken. While nearby their foe,
the wolf, once threatened, now again supreme,
prowls for prey and slays in bloodied snow,
        as geysers blow.

Good Dog

Why did he bring you here
to this place in the high desert?
Back home you jumped into the pickup, tail wagging,
excited about an adventure
as you had been a hundred times before.

    Good dog, stay.

You rode for hours and when he stopped
you were ready to run among the vermilion rocks.
But he didn't open the door.

    Good dog, stay.

The gun lay beside him on the seat.
You had seen it before but this time
something didn't seem right
so you whined ever so slightly.

    Good dog, stay.

The shot echoed inside the cab.
You had never liked loud noises.
His body jerked,
its essence escaping in a red river.
You whined more loudly now—even barked—
nudged him with your nose
but he just slumped in his seat,
his body stiff, then limp, not
hardly him at all.

    Good dog, stay.

For 40 days and nights you kept watch.
Jesus in the desert. Noah in the ark.
You only left your post
to jump through the half open window
to catch an occasional meal.

What selfishness made him bring you here
to witness his final act of cowardice,
so devoured by despair he couldn't see
your loyalty, itself reason enough to live?
Or was it just canine foolishness that made you

stay. Good dog.

(Boomers Driving) On the Taos Plateau
I'm not sleepy and there ain't no place I'm goin' to.
—Bob Dylan

Escaping Taos with its kitschy tourist shops and overpriced galleries
we drive west on US 64 across the Rio Grande Gorge
on the overarching "Most Beautiful Steel Bridge"
that spans this gash in the landscape,
now rusted and adorned with graffiti.
Memorials honor those who loved this place
as well as those for whom it was the last thing they saw.

We pass a subdivision of hobbit houses bermed into the desert—
Earthships off the grid and nearly out of sight
occupied by hybrids of survivalists and aging hippies.

Aspen embrace the serpentine road
as it undulates through residual snow drifts.
You sing a twangy nasal duet—half in mockery, half in homage—
with Bob Dylan on satellite radio
    Play a song for me
as we pretend the time is 40 years earlier
and our rented Ford Escape is a psychedelic Volkswagen bus
with gallon jugs of water in the back to feed the overheating engine,
long before anyone imagined GPS's or radio from satellites.
    In the jingle jangle morning I'll come following you.

In the Shadow of the Space Station

This is where we watch the stars
Kathryn says as she unlatches the gate
to the field. Four of us and the dog,
five no-longer-young revelers on a summer's night
spread blankets, open cabernet, pass paper cups.

Clouds part periodically to reveal a wisp of moon.
There it is someone cries.
But no, just Venus, that brazenly bright flirt
locked in her orbit.

Suddenly
Aeolus blows a hole in the clouds
to reveal infinite blackness punctuated by stars.

There is no mistaking the brilliance and the speed
as it arcs across the sky—
its trajectory confident, its crew oblivious to us below.

Perhaps the flautist astronaut is playing
while she floats weightless in the observation area,
looking down, admiring her blue planet.

As fact trumps the science fiction of our youth
you hold me tight
and I feel your silent tears
run down my still skyward-arching neck.

From Robert Frost's Porch

Pierced by the peak
of Mt. Lafayette
the full harvest moon
oozes lava
down the mist-enshrouded slope.

Open Mic at Luthier's

A single spotlight ricochets off the performers
onto a score of guitars-for-sale hung high on the wall.
It bounces off their high gloss and back into the crowd.
If you can call eight a crowd. In the dim light
the long list of local beers is unreadable
so you tell the girl with her hair hanging in her eyes
and the too turquoise eye shadow
to just pour you something light.

Guitar, harmonica and voice—that oldest of instruments—
blend in mesmerizing blues. The couple at the bar ignores
the musicians and each gropes
with one hand while texting with the other. The first,
lean in flannel shirt, workboots, her low-slung jeans revealing
a "tramp stamp." The other
in clingy black dress and ballet slippers. The girl behind the bar
pulls another beer. At the mic
middle age white accountants and professors
take turns living out their fantasies
as NOLA blues musicians. A hand slips into a waistband
blocking tattoos. A hand slides to the right
to rest where black dress and bar stool meet.
The song ends to light but appreciative applause.
The couple at the bar slips from their stools
and into the night.

How Maria Came to America

I.   *The Husband*

Because his wife had died
giving birth to their third child in as many years,
he sent for the sister. Though only 14
she had grown strong
farming the poor soil in the shadow of Mt. Vesuvius,
her already broad hips
designed by nature for the tasks ahead.

II. *The Crossing*

On the ship crammed with anxious
women and crying children,
her stomach echoed the heaving waves—
a harbinger of the sickness
which would wrack her young body
five times more in years to come.
But it was all right for
at the end of the journey her sister waited.
She thought.

III. *The Arrival*

At Ellis Island he told her,
and waited patiently
while she wept. When she had no more tears
for her dead sister, she gathered into her arms
the infant who had killed his mother
and sang to him softly in Italian.

According to Aunt Rose

No higher than the seatback of the patent leather limousine
that led them inexorably through the rites
of her brother's funeral,
the sardonic old woman spoke to her niece
with the prurient relish of a soap opera narrator
in a voice louder than was suitable—
attesting to both her hearing and her personality.

> *I'm the last one now that your father is dead.*
> *You should know how we got here.*
> *Grandpa had two wives.*
> *Our mother*
>   *—your father's and mine—*
> *was the second.*

As the limousine glided silently
the old woman mesmerized the mourners
with the story of a girl who,
      barely in her teens,
left her home in the shadow of Mt. Vesuvius
to visit her older sister in America.

> *They never told her*
> *that her sister had died in childbirth.*
> *They never told her*
> *that she was pledged to her sister's husband.*
> *They never told her.*

The old woman was silent
      and very far away.
When she returned she smiled mischievously,

> *My father was a horny old goat*
> *but my mother learned to love him.*

Euro Mutts

sons of Italy, daughters of Ireland
fleeing a continent overflowing with hate
where marches were not parades
where fireworks marked no celebration
escaping oppression, repression
trading bomb shelters and barbed wire
for stink of steerage, and heave of unseen sea

seduced by a verdigris-clad Siren whose song
lured them through her door of gold,
gold so plentiful it spilled into streets

streets that became canyons, walls formed by
paint-deprived tenements festooned with clotheslines
flapping to the music of crying infants
and a scent of garlic or borscht or any ingredient
that conjured up home and stanched the stench of free running sewers

disillusion, confusion
learning to respond to strange tongues
spitting out even stranger names—Wop, Mick, Kike—
with undisguised disgust

retreating to the familiar
seeking respite from a neighbor who could understand
and be understood

at night swathed in dreams of trees, hills, sky
dreams of distance and quiet,
and children running free, dreams
that for those children
there would be something more
than dreams

First Trip To New York
  —*for Lisa*

You and The Towers were only 5 or 6
when I took you there for your birthday.
Both so young. You ran around
the gleaming observation deck
on the 100th-something floor
leaping between stripes of sunlight
in your mint-green party dress. You shrieked—
then laughed—
when you spotted the tiny Statue of Liberty
below us in the harbor
amid the toy boats. I pointed to New Jersey
in the general direction of your house,
swallowed with its thousands of cousins
by the god Suburbia.
At the souvenir shop
you counted out change
from your pink plastic princess purse
to buy that little glass
with the red outline of The Towers.

I wonder what ever happened
to that glass.

Do NOT Stop for Hitchhikers

Fleeing North Jersey on Route 17
past numerous chrome diners
and precious few Priuses,
after yet one more funeral
where, like some fashion-conscious nun,
I had dressed in black Talbot's slacks and white T-shirt,
and a black raw silk jacket (Chico's),
and chatted politely with cousins I barely remembered
over a repast of bad pizza and worse wine.

I head due north, repelled by the City's negative pole,
ignoring my GPS's increasingly insistent directions
which would hurl me back into rush-hour stew
toward the dreaded I-95.
Finally she concedes and shuts up.

North toward mountains, away from traffic.
Set cruise control on 70. Take foot off gas.
Tune satellite to light rock. Exhale.
My blood pressure drops with a sigh.

Peekskill, Blauvelt, Haverstraw, Fishkill—
names along the valley become a chant
echoing my Dutch heritage. Correct
course at I-84 East. Thirty miles south
lies notorious Sing Sing,
renowned on *Law and Order*
where in 1910 an Italian immigrant "got the chair"
for killing his brother

who had bullied him once too often
for marrying a widow with six children
and promptly adding three more to the litter.

Beneath me the Hudson taunts
murmuring secrets I can never know.

Elegy for Palisades Amusement Park
1898 - September 12, 1971

> *After all is said and done*
> *It's Palisades for havin' fun.*
> *So during the day or when it's dark*
> *Visit this great amusement park.*
> *Skip the bother and skip the fuss*
> *[honk honk]*
> *Take a Public Service bus.*
> *Public Service sure is great*
> *It takes you right up to the gate.*
> —1960s radio ad

Named for neither corporate benefactor
nor cartoon mogul, but rather
for those rugged molten magma cliffs
which have towered above the Hudson since the Triassic,
your own time too brief even to register in the history of our planet.

From Google Earth the high-rise condominia
whose property values made you obsolete
form four massive white crosses marking your grave.
Do their shadowed alleys echo
with the laughter of generations of reveling ghosts?

Do you remember the embarrassment of the small girl
who cried so hard on the bumper cars
they had to stop in mid ride to let her leave?

Do you remember the name of the high-school boy
who brought that same girl to you on their first date, a virgin sacrifice?
The fun house blew air up her skirt,
a fledgling understudy for Marilyn Monroe in *The Seven Year Itch*.

Do you remember her last visit with The One?
a few years later and just before your demise?
He, terrified on the RoundUp, camera glued to his face,
hands trembling as he recorded your spinning lights.
She shrieking with abandon.

When rising property values forced you out
and you closed your gates that final day,
did you look across the Hudson to see the towers
gradually emerging from the skyline? You couldn't have known
30 years later they too would vanish.

The End of the Road

In the shadow of the Holyoke Range
along the seldom traveled dirt road
that floods impossibly impassable most Aprils
where cornfields meet forest
sits a tomato-colored GTO convertible. Top
permanently retracted or perhaps missing altogether,
golden maple leaves collect on its seats in fall,
snow in winter, a gaudy haven for mice.

Once proud muscle car of some young stud—
head turner, chick magnet, did he forsake you
for a practical minivan to load children? retriever? soccer gear?
Did you weary of the parade of macho young owners
who took all you could give for three decades,
more interested in appearance than maintenance,
and finally, when you no longer served their purpose,
abandoned you like some aging first wife?

Bandelier

> *On a summer night if you listen you can hear the drums by the ancient pueblo. My friend told me so, and I went and sat with her one night and I heard them too.*
> —Mestiza waitress at the Abiquiu Inn.

Stand quietly under the Corn Moon.
Do you hear the drums—
faint but there? In a long forgotten tongue
the old ones chant thanks for successful crops
that will stave off Winter's indifference.

Do you see them?
Faces of children peer out
from windows in the cliff
listening to the river's music
and watching the dancers' shadows
cast by the Moon.
Now that the harvest is in
tomorrow their father may have time
to draw another animal on the wall
to delight them—perhaps another strange bird
from his journey south.

Why did they flee this canyon
whose walls gave shelter?
whose river nurtured their crops?
What did they seek
that this Eden couldn't offer?

Meteor Crater, Arizona

Before the Diné or the Hopi or the Zuni
created the gods
so that the gods could create The People,

before the long robes came and christened
the home of The People's gods
with the name of their own patron saint,

while the woolly mammoth
and giant ground sloth
grazed grasslands in Pleistocene peace,

a fiery deity flew down from the sky
swifter, more powerful than those gods
who would dwell in the San Francisco Peaks.

The impact,
unlike any earth-bound animals
or gods had known,
punched a navel in the plains,
severing its flaming umbilical from the celestial belt
that gave the alien birth.

The unborn gods trembled
as their divine womb quaked.
Mammoths and sloths bellowed

then crept awestruck to the edge
of the flaming crucible to worship
this new, powerful god of heat and light.

The Weathervane

Bearing its swaddled burden
the ancient verdigris stork gyrates in the blizzard
above the roof of the vintage building
that once housed the nursery.

You sleep. I watch its frenzied dance
from beside your ICU bed.
How dare it flaunt a new life
as you fight for your old one.

Ephemeral white blankets the roof.
Functional white blankets your bed.
Life evanescent as April snow.
So much left unsaid. So much left undone.

Beeps and blips count off
seconds
        minutes
                hours
neon green lines undulate gently across a screen
reaffirming life
more fragile than a newborn infant
delivered by a whirling copper stork
in a blizzard.

Crossing the Lethe

Her son, the doctor,
of whom she had been so very proud,
now a stranger
no more alive to her than his stillborn sister
who would have been in her early forties.
He comes less frequently
now that she doesn't know him.

Friends stopped coming months ago
What's the use?

Sometimes forgetting at this age can be a blessing
coos the social worker
thinking what groceries she must buy
when her shift is finally over.

Take me home.

Tomorrow lies her husband
of more than five decades,
turning his head away.
Tomorrow he too is a stranger.
Yet he comes back.
        Yet he comes back.

Nurse! Nurse!
she screams trembling, tears glistening.
This woman—she keeps following me.

I know, but she won't hurt you
says the aide as she puts a hand on her shoulder
and gently guides her away
from the mirror.

The Hallway That Leads to the Morgue

Security doesn't really chill their beer there—
that's just a little gallows humor.
Deep in the hospital basement
through double doors marked
"employees only"
past those stepchildren of health care—
the laundry with its pulsing machines
churning through never ending mountains
of linens and blue and white johnnies,
past the print shop with its thumping press
churning out guidelines and newsletters.

The walls aren't decorated. Someone tried
to paint the cinder block years ago—
that institutional green—now dingy and flaking.
And no one has bothered to camouflage
the steam pipes that run the length of the ceiling
making it much warmer than you'd expect.

There is no signage. The living who need to go there
know where it is and carry out their work
somberly and quickly. They are on their way
to that place where dreams disappear,
far below the floors where life begins or is renewed.
Far below the rooms where hope endures.

The Boy Up the Street

I.

Your feet barely reached the pedals
as you skidded your hand-me-down bike into my driveway
that Saturday in May
while I crouched weeding around spring bulbs.

How much? you asked
pointing to my glorious yellow Darwins.
For your Mom? I asked.
Never big on words, you nodded.
Take them.
You shook your determined head.
How much?
OK then, a nickel.

You dug the coin out of your pocket,
passed it to me with grimy hands.
I picked a half dozen of the choicest.

You laid them carefully in your bike's rusting basket
and rode back to the ramshackle farmhouse
that loomed at the top of the hill,
its paint long gone.

II.

I woke to sirens one January night
a decade later. That now-abandoned farmhouse
cast a sunset glow on the crest of the hill
permeating nearby yards and woodlots.
As flames devoured century-old clapboards
orange ghosts danced mockingly in window frames.
Ice caked firefighters and hoses
while engines groaned with exertion.

As your childhood home died that night
did you turn restlessly
on your Army-issued cot
in some godforsaken sandtrap?
or were you dreaming of yellow tulips?

The Lupines of Ushuaia

in January for God's sake
almost at the bottom of the earth

improbable purples, pinks, blues, magentas
oblivious to steely sea or leaden mountains

prized specimen of Yankee gardeners
or riotous wild children running unbridled on northern hillsides

in May, early June perhaps
but never in January

turning the planet upside down
almost at its God forsaken bottom

what seeds from above earth's belt found their way here
what hubris or optimism marked their sowing
what lust their fecundity

Overheard in the Quiet Car

Grampa. Don't fall for any of those people who play the guitar in the subway. Don't pay them. They all have jobs. Grampa. Grampa. Hey the train's even taller than that roof. Why did we stop? Grampa, why did we stop? Grampa do the cars get more dirty when they go fast or when they go slow? I'm on page 400 Grampa. Hey lookit the sharks Grampa. Hey lookit the blood. Big train. The Empire State Building. Why do they call it the Statue of Liberty Grampa? Why do they call it that? Hey Grampa look. We're going over water. Hope we don't fall in. Hey lookit. Word things. Wanna do it? Oh. It's already done. How much longer? Are we in New York yet? It doesn't matter. How come we keep picking up more people? We just keep going round and round in a circle until we get there. How many stations are there? I lost track.

In fifth grade Mrs. van Stone suggested to **Marianne** that she should consider a career in writing. Coming from a pragmatic family, that translated to pursuing a journalism degree, which she did at the Newhouse School at Syracuse University. After several stints on daily and weekly newspapers, she escaped New Jersey to live in the verdant Pioneer Valley of Western Massachusetts, where the cultural life is as lush as the farms, and where she worked in public relations for a nonprofit arts organization.

Her poems have been published in several print and online journals including *The Aurorean, The Copperfield Review, Oberon Poetry Magazine, Pirene's Fountain, Avocet Journal, Snowy Egret* and *The Naugatuck River Review*. Her essay "The Labyrinth at Kripalu" appeared in *Touch: The Journal of Healing*. Not wanting to abandon her journalistic roots entirely, she writes occasional columns for the *Daily Hampshire Gazette* (Northampton, MA) and serves on the scholarship committee for the Valley Press Club.

She is a member of the Florence Poets Society and serves on the editorial team for their annual journal, *Silkworm*; and is a member of the Monson Poets and the Quabbin Writers Salon. After trying on a number of writers' conferences, she found a home at the annual Green Mountain Writers Conference, where she found both friendship and confidence. When she is not gardening, her volunteer work at the local community hospital and regional humane society gives her endless fodder for her writing. She lives in a 150+ year-old farmhouse with her husband, Jim, a fine art photographer, and three feline critics.
https://margampoetry.wordpress.com

www.ingramcontent.com/pod-product-compliance
Lightning Source LLC
LaVergne TN
LVHW041511070426
835507LV00012B/1491